Garlands and Laurels

Sharelle Moyer

Garlands and Laurels
by
Sharelle Mayer

Limited Edition

Illustrations by
Brenda Alpinieri

Calligraphy by
janet grosser

Prologue Publications
Menlo Park, California

ISBN Number: 0-930048-08-3
Library of Congress Number: 79-91323

Inquiries should be addressed to:

Prologue Publications
P.O. Box 640
Menlo Park, CA 94025

To my Parents,
Shari and Herb Mayer

Contents

Preface

I think of all the perspectives we have during our lifetimes and of all the melodies, but the incident that suggested *Garlands and Laurels* was a rather hectic tennis game one May and a cool lemonade at a composer friend's house. He was a pianist and he played this piece by Noel Coward:

> *"I'll see you again, whenever spring breaks through again. Time may lie heavy between—but what has been—is past forgetting. The sweet memory, across the years, will come to me; tho' my world may go awry, in my heart will ever lie, just the echo of a sigh, good-bye."**

SM

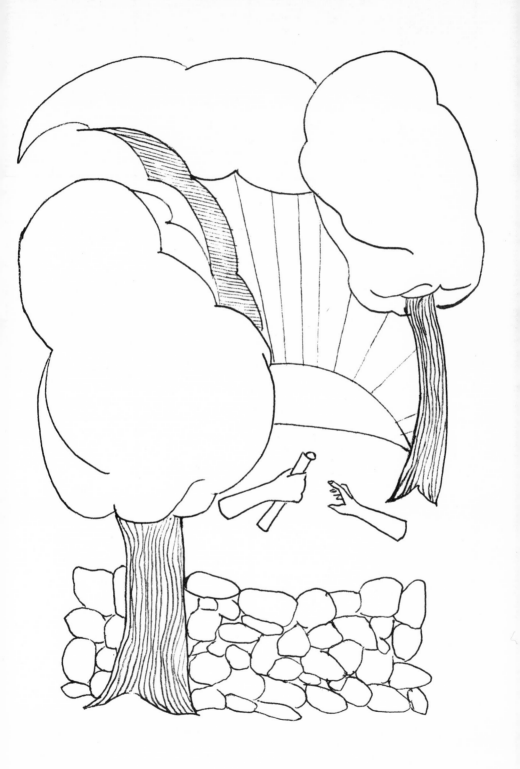

Garlands and Laurels

The Orchard

I was sitting among the graduation guests on one of the rented folding chairs on the hockey field. I was there because my godchild, Barbara Marie Simmons, was graduating from the eighth grade. The Orchard was my school too, since I had gone there many years ago. Yet, there was a lot more to The Orchard now than there ever was then.

The ceremony started. *Pomp and Circumstance* came over the loud-speakers. The graduating Lower School in their summer party dresses paraded traditionally down the middle of the horseshoe-arranged guest chairs, flanked by their garlands of dark green leaves, softened by white gardenias.

I thought of the garlands of The Orchard—how much had happened, how much was the same and how much was different. I think I was beginning to feel like a photographic proof that had had too much of the sun's rays and was beginning to fade.

I looked at the program of the Lower and Upper School graduates. The list of names for both was printed so everyone was mentioned. Some even had special asterisks after their names, denoting the laurels of special achievements. My graduation class had twelve girls and no asterisks. We just got our diplomas. There were no plaques, cups or prizes. We had our copy of *The Branch*, the school's yearbook, autographed by friends and teachers and the pages would be polka dotted with syrupy, pink punch.

After today's graduation, there would be wine, apple cider, cookies and pleasantries and school history would be made. The sisterhood had been extended to man and the first boys to graduate would be receiving a certificate of completion from The Orchard.

I looked around and could see the parade of seniors starting to form. Did we have girls that tall in our class or ones so well drilled in finding their places on the raised platform? It was the boys who looked awkward this year. It must have been hard for them to start in at an established, all girl's school.

The sun shown brightly and was beginning to cook my section of chairs. I couldn't help but nod off to other times but not other places.

"Well, here's The Orchard, Caroll," Mother said, as she drove up to the late Renaissance-style mansion. "Go in and get your uniform list and your bus schedule. Why you want to go to this school so far from home with people who won't be living in your neighborhood is beyond me!"

"I told you and Dad that the school is only five years old and it doesn't have boarders. It's designed to help all kinds of students. I haven't been learning anything in public school. All we had was one report on Paul Revere and recess—except for listening to the World Series with the boys on the classroom science radio."

"All right, Caroll; your father and I have told you that we'd let you give it a try but I don't think you'll like going to school in Hillview as well as you would in Palo Alto."

"Yes, I will! I'll like it better because it's newer and..." I think I wanted to say that I might be able to graduate with an asterisk if I had known of such things but I was out the car door and popping in through the entrance to the main building.

I stood a little dumb-founded in the wide reception hall and remembered that I wanted to see the forbidding Miss Brook, Headmistress. I waited for a minute or two outside her office and then I saw her. I was sure she was a leftover World War I Red Cross Volunteer. She wore her silver hair pulled back into a bun and seemed pleased to see me again through her steel-rimmed spectacles. She'd given me the entrance examinations a few weeks earlier.

I was always very courteous to Miss Brook because Mother had said that she was a "Lady." I might have added "old" to that but I wasn't a hotshot then. I was only beginning a new life and like a newborn foal, feeling for my balance.

After my freshman year was beyond midpoint, there were a number of derogatory remarks made about Miss Brook by the other students. I still liked my first impression and stuck with it until one of my classmates came up with a better one. Betsy Kandy said she wore her dresses so long that they hung on her like she used two slingshots to hold up her boobs instead of a bra.

Miss Brook had been at the school for six years as the first Headmistress when the school was originally in a small church hall in San Mateo. She had done the recruiting of the staff and students. Now it looked as if the school was building up its growth and girth in the bank and she would retire.

I'm really very vague as to all of the situations or what she actually did that year besides post a list of "No-No's." Outstanding has to be her starting off every morning with Assembly, the saying of the Lord's Prayer *and being just what Mother said, a "Lady" Headmistress.*

Where did that breeze come from? Oh, the procession is almost over. There go the last of the faculty mortar boards and black gowns with the satin ribbons of graduation distinctions from previous commencements. They are beating it down the old Chisholm Trail for another year as Orchard teachers. Too many for me now to try to guess what subjects they specialized in but more than one third are younger than I am. Some I recognize from the alumnae newsletter's photos and write-ups but there are many that I will never know and some I've missed. Here come the Board of Trustees, all having one thing in common besides fund-raising: they are going to sit in the sun and not move and look forward to a tall, cool drink when the last diploma is handed out.

Today is Barbara's day. Thirteen years old, wearing a pretty white linen and white-embroidered, square-necked dress, she is going on twenty-three. She's already announced that if she continues at The Orchard, it will be only because they eliminate the uniform; otherwise, she's going to go to Los Altos High School and wear casual stuff. (I've deciphered this and it comes out blue jeans.) Barbara is a cute girl, popular, and a leader among her peers in pointing out that if the boys don't have to wear uniforms why should the girls and if there are boys at school, why shouldn't the girls wear what they want to? She is decisively an equal rights promoter.

Uniforms—the pleated skirts of yellow and gray plaid

with ever the slightest trace of red fleck in the wool, the white blouses, the yellow sweaters and the Oxford gray blazer with its yellow crest of The Orchard, a tree with spreading branches of metallic gold thread. Now, a twenty-five year old misappropriation if they let the trends of the times submerge one of the most distinguished aspects of The Orchard's life. Maybe the convenience of yesteryear, not having to decide what to wear to class, is the inconvenience of today. At best, I'm glad I'm not Barbara Marie—having to show off her adolescent personality through clothes and snubbing the practicality of school uniforms. I wonder what I did with my old blazer's crest? I'm sure I saved it but where did I put it?

There's a crackling sound coming over the public address system. All are in their places on the platform. A senior girl of medium height and fair blond hair, wearing her pale blue cap and gown, is coming to the podium. My goodness! We're going to be welcomed. A little more practice at talking into the microphone might have made her invocation and poetry a bit more audible. Let's see; she was Patty Cantwell, Student Body President and across from her name, the alphabetized list shows her going to UCLA.

The colleges and universities chosen by the graduating seniors are varied. I wonder how many will finish their four years, or transfer, or get married, or do both or just... well. The list of acceptances certainly reads like a glamorous roll call of hard work, worthy recommendations and individual awareness.

I don't see anyone going to any of my alma maters for undergraduate work—not big enough or traditional enough, I suppose. Out of a class of thirty-six this year, five chose Stanford and five the University of California at Berkeley. It seemed the boys who didn't go back east chose Cal and they'll all probably make a fraternity. Such fun they'll all have with The Orchard's preparation to lead them out into the world along with their parent's padding. I can wish them the best.

There is someone at the podium now, the guest speaker, a prominent, local resident who had served as state representative in Washington, D. C. She is telling the Upper and Lower School graduates of the myriad of opportunities they have to render service to their country, state, city, neighbors and how to make living life an educational thing by being grandly involved with social causes, science, research and the arts.

Gads! She is convincing. All each and every one of those graduates has to do is step out of his or her front door the next day and her wind will have each one of them positioned as a civic leader with a capital "C" and a capital "L." I guess that when you are sitting and waiting to receive your diploma, maybe you don't always hear the speech of the day, but this one was sure a pip.

I could do no better, even with twenty years hindsight, addressing a body of teenage graduates. But I know my godchild is thinking more about her class' hot-tub party than about goals for America. Her diploma and the party are the marks on her growth chart, proof that she is becoming more independent and developing a very outstanding personality.

Yet, if she got a morsel from the address it would probably have been the equality of brotherhood that was eventually mentioned. Barbara knew no color barrier, nor did The Orchard. I observed the sprinkling of black and Oriental students who were getting their diplomas today.

"What's that!" The lady sitting next to me had nudged me and asked me if I was an alumna.

"Why, yes; is it noticeable?" I said.

She smiled and asked me if there was a misprint in

the program or if the Headmaster's name was really Richard Lovebird.

I whispered, "That's true; his name is Lovebird and he's pretty good. Tough job being Headmaster of a private school," I said as he started to ramble on monosyllabically and then I added, "Do you know one of the graduates here today?"

"Yes, my niece is graduating, Susan Brett, and I've come all the way from Santa Cruz."

"How nice," I replied while adjusting my straw sun hat and noticed that the prizes were now being handed out.

Richard Lovebird, that struck a note, I thought. When it was announced in the newsletter that a *man* was appointed Headmaster of The Orchard, an all girl's school, it was the clue that it wasn't going to be long before co-education was in the classrooms and it wasn't—only four years. There really wasn't anything wrong with him as a Princeton graduate but that didn't necessarily mean there was anything right with him either. A man of compromise and dullness. He made his points and covered his tracks—a man of the moment.

So what difference did it make? The students all liked him and everyone is entitled to his expression. I just missed the Headmistresses that I was schooled under after "The World War I Red Cross Volunteer." They were a little more fiery...

Gee! It's the same at every graduation. The same names get called on to come up and get their honors. If I had to sit there on the platform as an unprized student and watch others garner their laurels while I had my hands folded in my lap, empty, I think I would make faces at them as they came back to their seats.

Let's see now. Lee Chinn has taken one plaque, four wrapped up packages (books, I suppose) for being an outstanding student. Here comes Patty Cantwell again. She's just gotten the "General Excellence Award."

I wonder why they don't give out awards to distinguished alumnae? The school is so young, I guess. Well, let's see; we could have one for the person having the most children, the biggest house and the most volunteer jobs. Another voice from the mirage. "Caroll, you're being facetious!"

"I know."

"What's that?" the lady from Santa Cruz said.

"My goodness," I replied. "Do you wonder when they'll get to the passing out of diplomas?"

"Oh, yes. My niece, Susan Brett, is going to the party at Lakeside tonight."

"Yes, I heard about that. My godchild is graduating from the eighth grade and having the class party at her house in Los Altos."

"Lakeside, with a live band..." she hemmed.

Well, the five o'clock sun was releasing itself and I think the audience was with it as Mr. Lovebird introduced the President of the Board of Trustees to do the conferring of diplomas. He was a handsome, over-ruddied, healthy man.

Let's see...he hands out the diplomas to the Lower School first. I mustn't miss Barbara's acceptance and know she'll not pass out or trip on the way to getting her certificate.

My, this is taking no time at all. Barbara got her diploma with the blue ribbon and now they are passing out the Upper School's diplomas with yellow ribbons. There certainly seems to be a unanimity to this. Everyone appears happy and smiling. I think it must be that even the ones who had the hardest times getting through their final examinations feel equal to the ones who received special achievement awards.

As I watch this applauded convoy of individuals, I can't help remembering the many years ago when I got up and got my diploma. My feelings about receiving it and about graduation didn't initiate tears at that moment, only relief and a feeling of how lucky I was. In my class at The Orchard, there were those who broke like a bottle and cried during the Recessional. As I remember it now, it was during the Recessional that most of the class members were in tears. One would start, and then another and by the time we gathered about our parents and friends, there seemed to be an epidemic. It must have been the generation.

Now we're invited to join in the school hymn. It's not a *You'll Never Walk Alone* but I do like the part *Where new horizons call the mind, the choice is ours to search and find.* I think I'm going to find the blue skies above and, hopefully, Barbara's mother, Pat, who said she liked to sit in the back. I'll also look around and see if I know anyone.

The Orchard's hocky field was drenched by a march of Tchaikovsky's pouring through the loud-speakers. The Recessional had begun. The audience got up from their folding chairs and followed the general mode of dismissal, moving towards the school's large brick terrace.

In the back, steps from the green grass of the field led up to the terrace. Once there, the guests were aroused with trays of apple cider and cookies. Trays, covered with plastic glasses of warm, white chablis, one-third filled, were set out on long tables. The activity was like bees swarming but there just weren't the same number of familiar faces from the past.

"Hi." It was Barbara tugging at my elbow.

"Congratulations. Let's see your diploma," I greeted her and then added, "Where's your mom?"

Barbara opened the simulated leather pass book and under isinglass was her certificate from The Orchard. Pat had found us and was now hugging Barbara. I opened my purse to give Barbara her graduation card and check.

"Here's a little something for you," I said. Barbara opened the card and took the pale yellow check out first thing. She handed it to her mother with, "This is for the bank." She was my godchild all right. Then she looked at me as if there should be something else.

"Barbara, do you still have the *Saturday Night Fever* album I gave you?"

"Yes, I do, and we're going to play it at the party tonight but it sticks on side one."

"Well, I hope you have ear plugs for your mother," I said looking at Pat, in a light, pink wool dress and pearls.

"Oh, I'm used to it," she said, sounding almost as though nothing ever really bothered her. Pat was a widow, an old friend of the family since the time her husband was alive.

"Well, why don't we have some refreshments and then I think I will have to be going." I said.

I caught the eye of one of the servers and she brought over a tray filled with glasses of wine. Pat and I each took one. Barbara left looking for her classmates and some cider.

"Why do you have to leave? Heavy date tonight?" Pat said, grinning.

"No, not anything major. Michael is coming by for our mid-week backgammon game and I'm cooking dinner."

"How long have you been dating Michael, Caroll, and when is the wedding? I want to be there and Barbara would make a lovely little bridesmaid," she said seriously.

"Oh, well, don't hold your breath. One reason why Michael and I have gone together for so long is that we really don't think about marriage," I said trying to get her off the track.

Barbara joined us and said she couldn't find any cider and that she didn't really want anything but a coke anyway.

"Well, we have plenty of that at home. I've got three cases of pop and enough hot dogs and potato chips for Barbara's eighteen classmates who are coming to the party tonight," Pat said, as if she was planned out, but enthused for Barbara.

"Do you have a cake?" I said.

"Yes, ordered from the Los Altos bakery and strawberry ice cream. I hope that you and Michael will come by." Pat winked.

"It sounds too good to pass up. Maybe we will. Well, I think I'd better get cracking."

"Yes, we'll have to go too as soon as Barbara gets back," she said, watching Barbara throw our empty plastic wine glasses into a container at a corner of the terrace.

"Well, see ya soon," I said, and turned to leave, running into Barbara on my way.

"Have a great time tonight," I said, happy for Barbara. She smiled back at me.

Upon leaving The Orchard, there was always a long walk to the car and I thought of what Pat said about coming to my wedding...she'd been asking me that same question for fifteen years—before Barbara was born. Oh well, that was Pat.

Too bad I didn't see any alumnae whom I would have enjoyed saying hello to. Well, there would always be the fundraising party in the fall.

Gads! These cars are really packed around this small driveway. I guess I'll have no trouble getting mine out.

I looked back at The Orchard and saw the white building with its three stories and porte-cochere entrance. I remember when it was covered with ivy, before the ivy had decayed and the vines removed. The building had been sandblasted clean and it sparkled in the early evening sheen.

Pulling Weeds

Have you ever seen someone pull a weed and make it look like the easiest thing this side of scooping up sand with a small shovel? Traveling through my memories of The Orchard, I come to this recollection of Mrs. Lassen.

She wasn't a headmistress, a teacher or a member of the staff and I don't even know her first name. She was a parent. It was an added dimension that her husband was on the original Board of Trustees but freshmen students such as I never bothered putting those facts together. Why she, more than any other parent, did so much volunteer work to see that the school had a decent landscape, I just didn't know.

I had heard that she had two daughters in attendance at the school and that she lived down the hill from The Orchard. Today I believe that she would have been the same unassuming, helpful, concerned person, donating much of her time to parent groups and other causes with or without her car, on a bicycle if she wanted, for she appeared neatly frugal.

But her car then was rather noticeable: a British, racing green Jaguar (model XK150, I think). I remember seeing it parked to one side of the school building with the trunk open. At recesses, I watched her direct the school's gardeners to the planting areas that she felt needed to be cleaned out, removing the shrubs that had withered so they could plant her orange blossom bushes. I saw her in a jean skirt, white blouse and red cardigan sweater pull weeds and also give a lot of new form to the old, more formal landscaping around The Orchard.

Today, I think Mrs. Lassen would probably have liked to have been a landscape architect professionally. In my mind she is. She is also a very youngish grandmother, one who has had the pleasure of seeing her daughters' children go on to the same school that she gave so much to.

Mrs. Lassen wasn't very tall, a little less than medium height. She had dark brown eyes. Her brunette hair was cut in a bob, an easy wave over her forehead. She never looked anything but happy to meet you and see you and never worried about the time or weather conditions. She was adherent to her space.

My first meeting with "the landscape architect" took place in November. The late morning fog had turned into a drizzle by lunch. I had gotten half-way down the hill from The Orchard with my books, walking in the direction of the downtown train station when she drove by me, slowed her car and waited. When I got even with the car, her window went down.

She said, "Do you need a ride?"

I remembered everything my mother had told me about not taking rides from strangers but the Jaguar didn't seem to be a stranger. I drooped a little and said, "It's probably out of your way."

"Where do you want to go?" She was getting more to

the point.

"I'm on my way home. I'm going to take the train. Are you going downtown?"

"Yes, I'm going that way."

I walked over to the passenger's side of the car, opened the door and got in.

"You're from The Orchard, aren't you?" she said, surveying my uniform and books. "What's your name?"

"Caroll Dwy..." but before I could finish pronouncing my last name, she said,

"I have two daughters at The Orchard."

"What are their names?" I said.

She turned a corner and I got a good look at the Jag's instrument panel. It was paneled in wood and the instruments were all in round circles, unusual for a 1950's car. I guess it was the first Jaguar I'd ever been in. I took such an inventory that I didn't hear whether she told me her daughters' names or not. The radio softly tuned to an especially melodic station was not helping my attention either.

"Do you always take the train home from school?"

Here it was, a hint that she knew I was cutting out from the afternoon study schedule.

"No, not always but I didn't feel well today and the school bus doesn't get me to Atherton until late," I said, beginning to enjoy the comfortable, all leather interior.

Mrs. Lassen stopped at a light, looked at me and said, "Do you like The Orchard?"

I answered honestly and said, "Yes, but I don't have too many friends and there isn't too much to do in the afternoons except study hall and I wish that we had more intramural sports programs."

The light changed and she followed the stream of traffic downtown towards the railroad station.

"Oh, you don't have to take me to the station. I can get out anywhere along here," I said, grabbing at my books for an easy exit.

"I have to go this way, anyway," she said and then slowly added, "My little boy loves Chinese food and I'm going to pick some up right around the corner from where you are going."

"Oh, then there is no problem," I said.

"No problem at all," she assured me.

I felt relaxed and finally asked, "Aren't you Mrs...?"

"Mrs. Lassen," she replied.

I was quiet as a clam the next three blocks and thrilled with her telling me her name. I even knew, now, for sure, who her daughters were. Gads! What a day! In fact, when she pulled over to the passengers unloading curb at the station, the sun was doing one of its peek-a-boos through the clouds.

I rode the train and thought I must tell Jan and Rebecca tomorrow what a nice Mother they have and that I had met her.

The next day I was encompassed with the rest of the school's attendance. However, I searched out Jan Lassen. I met her in the hallway of the second floor during a break in class periods. She was a year older than I. I mentioned meeting her mother and that I was Caroll Dwyer from Atherton. Jan, short and slight, didn't seem impressed or unimpressed but interested to know where I was at The Orchard. My class status as a freshman and that I rode the bus seemed to click somewhere but she was a sophomore with direction and didn't have time. She was pleasant and said she hoped I would get involved with the elective programs.

I thought, "Jan talks...she talked to me—at least that's starting somewhere." When I found Rebecca Lassen during

((18))

morning break in the dining room on the first floor, most all of us were indulging in cookies and milk snacks. Rebecca, a year younger than I, was taller than her sister and very thin. She didn't listen to me and grimaced and moved acrobatically. It was enough to deflate my whole day. Oh, what the heck! Rebecca was only an eighth grader; she wouldn't be that way next year.

I gave considerable thought to what Jan said about electives. I was in chorus. I sat and sang but didn't know anyone there. I decided to change my seat next to someone in my class.

Towards the end of November, Mrs. Lassen stopped working in the gardens. She was among a surveying team that was going to create a basketball court. The word was out at Assembly that construction was going to begin and we were not to play in that area until it was completed.

Mrs. Lassen drove up each day and met with the contractors. The area was cleaned of brush and rough graded by a light Caterpillar bulldozer. I saw this from the window of the first floor library. What was going on outside those windows was more fascinating to me than what was going on inside during this daily construction. The next few days, the area was finish graded and leveled with a light motor grader and then compacted by a steel wheel roller.

As time went by, we, who were noticing, were saying, "Hope it doesn't rain so we can have our basketball court." It didn't and after the Thanksgiving weekend, a small paver spread the asphalt surfacing and we watched it until it had been rolled for the proper asphalt compaction. What was even more fun than watching the progress was seeing the basketball court being properly marked with a small line marker.

The backboards and basket hoops were erected by a light, truck-mounted crane. On that day, both Mr. and Mrs.

Lassen were there to supervise. Then the finishing touch of bleacher seats being constructed by the crane on either side of the basketball court even got Miss Brook away from her math class blackboard to see it.

It looked as though there was going to be an option to hockey on the lawn and indoor gymnastics in the basement. They even had the asphalt marked off for a tennis court. There were a lot of lines on that surface but in the early days of a school's growth, there is often a making do with what you've got.

Meanwhile, I had found a new chair in chorus, near the front, around the fourth row next to a pleasant blonde who lived in Hillview and smiled a lot. She had a sparkle in her eyes and told me that she liked my haircut. I could have said the same about hers as we both wore our hair the same length and it was about the same color. Her name was Betsy Kandy.

Chorus was held in one-half of an L-shaped room next to the library. There was a spinet piano, a section of chairs on the left for alto range and a section of chairs on the right for soprano range. Betsy and I were both altos. She preferred wearing the Oxford blazer to the sweater just as I did.

We were practicing a program for the upcoming Christmas show and one day we burst out laughing to each other when the pianist did her introduction to *Walking in a Winter Wonderland.* It seemed that no matter how many times Mrs. Ford, our choral director, told her accompanist to start at a certain stanza, the pianist had to do the complete introduction to the song, which completely broke up Betsy and me. We could always feel the same bars of music coming on and knew exactly which way the accompanist was going to sway and swing with her introduction before she got to the certain part that Mrs. Ford was interested in rehearsing. Gads! We laughed at that jolly piano player! She worked harder at her introduction than she did with the rest of the piece. The rest of the song was peppermint compared to her introduction which was divinity.

The school did put on the Christmas show for parents and Betsy began to telephone me in the evenings to check out homework assignments. We both detested algebra and liked English. I think I liked more about the school than she did because she was always more bugged about something than I was. We were good friends although we lived in separate towns.

During the Christmas vacation, she came down to my house. We decorated the tree and took my dog for a walk. The area was tree-filled, with rambling California ranch homes sitting on acre lots. Betsy showed me the house her parents had lived in before they had moved to Hillview. It was a block away from my house.

We sure looked like the Bobbsey twins, wool Bermuda shorts, blouses, pull-over sweaters and red Bermuda socks with loafers. But Betsy was full of the "to Hell with school" routine and I didn't know what she was getting at. She gave me an encased Japanese doll for Christmas. I gave her an ashtray since we both smoked. The only difference being she could smoke in her bedroom and I had to smoke outside while walking the dog, not in front of my parents.

Betsy was shoving it down my way, over the phone, pretty heavily about how unhappy she was at The Orchard and how she really wanted to go to public high school. I would say "Well, why don't you?" She would repeat that she had friends at the local high school, mostly boys, and that The Orchard wasn't helping her social life. I could do nothing but agree with her on that point.

By March, Betsy had me dropping by her house in Hillview on Friday afternoons. Her house was larger as it was a two-story French chateau style. It wasn't more than twenty-five years old; it just appeared more classical than mine. We had poolside clambakes but no clams—just potato chips and beer and boys. I would take an evening train home, explaining to my parents that I was at Betsy Kandy's and that we had sunned around the pool.

Sunned around the pool was right! One afternoon there were four boys older than we and it was heaven (freshman year talking). It seems to me that Betsy and I and her admirers had one beer and decided to give Betsy's German shepherd, Robby, a beer and see what he would do. We did, poured one bottle into his large dog dish. Nothing much happened except he lapped it up, crossed his paws and put his head down on top of them. We howled with laughter. One of the guys suggested that we toss him into the pool. Betsy said, "No," but then said, "to sober him up, OK."

The boys pulled and pushed and finally wound up carrying the dog to the coping of the pool near the steps. With a great toss, they threw Robby into the pool. The dog paddled to the side.

I said, "The dog doesn't know where the steps are and someone should get him out."

Betsy said, "Robby knows where the steps are; just give him time."

Sure enough, Robby found the steps, pranced out and shook himself off. He was eyeing us all with "It's tough to lead the life of a dog."

The four boys were enamored of Betsy. I could see that I didn't have a chance and left for my walk to the train station and the Friday evening train. But, gads! What a day! Betsy's mother was never home much, like mine, but *I* could never have pulled off such an extravaganza. I didn't know four boys (older)... and, I didn't know how to get the beer...

and, I would never dream of giving any to my faithful mutt.

My parents had a pool. As far as I was concerned, it was for adult parties and barbecues. Also, it offered scenic beauty but it wasn't meant for after school high jinks. I was really just a cigarette-smoking square.

I guess I was the *Paper Moon* for Betsy because she only attended The Orchard that freshman year and never called me again.

Biology 10

When The Orchard opened its doors to a new autumn semester, it also had a new Headmistress, Miss DiSalvo, who had formerly been the Assistant to the Dean of Women at Stanford. She was making the office in the Gothic style library on the first floor her place. Coming from there into the main hallway was a constant curl of smoke floating out through the open, hand-carved, wooden door.

Miss DiSalvo was the skirt and blouse type. She wore low heeled shoes and smoked filter tip cigarettes. She was the intellectual type with understanding and compassion for most daily psychological problems. I remember about six weeks into the term Tracy said that there should be a tin cup placed outside her door with a sign that read, "Psychological Help, 5¢."

True, when any of the seniors or juniors had problems or decision-making blocks, Miss DiSalvo would close the door and be "in conference." There were always some students who opted to talk to Miss DiSalvo rather than go to physical education or take a study hall. Evidently, they must have gotten a lot of help, as most everyone who had a conference with the Headmistress felt better about something than when she had gone in.

Nothing was ever enforced about the rule of "no smoking in the school uniform." By this time, there were about eight to ten girls, who, during recess break, would gather from where they might be and head downstairs towards the front door. I was among the several in the smoking herd. As regular as clockwork, we would have our ciggies in one hand and match or lighter in the other. We would parade out the double door and walk behind the bushes—as if one could miss seeing the clouds of smoke rise above the shrubbery, as it was all, really, in plain view.

It certainly was a mystery that the smoking herd was obvious to everyone but the smokers. Miss DiSalvo never said a word to any of us individually but made casual mention of the no smoking rule at Assembly as if none of The Orchard students smoked. I can remember her topping off a sentence with, " ..and there is no smoking on the school grounds." The way she said it made it about as effective as if she had said, "...and there will be no gum chewing in class," or "... and there will be no chocolate sundae for dessert today."

Smoking cigarettes led me to Tracy Douglas. She was a year younger than I but she smoked and had two older brothers who had taught her a lot of words and told her a lot of jokes that I had never heard before. Tracy was coarse, overweight and comical as hell. It all seemed to enhance her personality and made it most definite. She also rode the school bus to Atherton and we discovered early in September that we lived six blocks from each other. Ever since that day we rode the bus together and gossiped, joked, complained and went to the rear of the bus every afternoon to have a cigarette after most of the other students were let off. Most of the complaints that we had centered around having to ride the bus. Most of our jokes were plays on words. Tracy would say, "Did you know that 'God' spelled backwards is 'dog'?"

I'd say, "No, but my father thinks he sees Him in church."

Tracy would laugh at what I'd say and I'd laugh at what she said. But the gossip Tracy poured out was mostly about Miss DiSalvo's conference sessions and who was going into the Gothic office and sitting on the couch the most often. I really didn't care. It was no business of mine but it seemed to fascinate Tracy.

What did fascinate me was biology. It was the first time I'd ever had a science class.

In public school we had a science book called *The How and Why Club* which remained unopened on the bookshelves in the back of the schoolroom. I was looking forward to Biology 10.

This intriguing science lecture and laboratory course was taught by Miss Fair. She was from the east coast and had done little teaching but had excellent credentials from Swarthmore, among them a physical education certificate. She also was The Orchard's hockey and basketball teacher. She liked hockey best of the sports, even had her own hockey stick. Biology held no interest for her. She was teaching her pupils as if they were an opposing team that she had to stay ahead of at all times.

There were two biology classes and laboratory periods. Because of my schedule, I was placed in the afternoon class with members of the junior and senior classes. The classroom laboratory was in the basement of the building with high windows that let little light into the room. Hence, there were fluorescent lights hanging from the ceiling which would hopefully flood the classroom into a timeless zone of scientific concentration. I know that I often thought of these lights as my only aid, since the students didn't pair up to do any of the reports, quizzes or lab reports. Each student was on her own. However, I did notice that in the rear of the classroom where the second door and the older students were, there was more table talk than where I was in the class, first row, center. I sat there so as best to see the blackboard and follow directions.

I did follow directions. I drew from eye to hand—concentrated freestyle—a microscope and labeled all of its parts and learned their functions. I had never drawn any object by looking at it; I wasn't an art student. However, in Miss Fair's class, it was becoming clear that any artistic qualities would be very helpful. If anything, it did help handwriting dexterity. I had gotten back a check mark and the advice to try to keep handwriting and labeling within the guidelines. So, I also was beginning to see where calligraphy would be helpful.

The class spent a lot of time looking at vegetable and mineral substances under the microscope. As I remember, it all had to do with protoplasm and living cells versus those substances that didn't carry on life functions. I think we spent three weeks on discovering the cells of vegetable and animal substances and diagnosing them. I was there drawing all these new microscopic slides onto a thick, white sheet of paper with all the proper labeling and just when I thought I'd get a check mark with a plus, there would be some comment like: "Wrong side of the paper" and a simple, single check mark.

Finally, after doing cross sections of plant roots and carrots and looking at the structure of plant stems, we did what I'm sure all biology classes do. We put a collection of leaves together and analyzed them. Also, in this series of lessons, we learned about photosynthesis.

It was at about this time that I was doing a little root

making of my own. I often bicycled over to Tracy's house after school with my dog running alongside. I would ring the doorbell explaining that I was out giving Julie her run. Tracy was never too busy to see me. We played with the dog and then I'd bicycle back home. However, it wasn't too much longer that I'd just bike on over to Tracy's and not bring my dog and was told to "come on in; the door's open." I'd become a regular member of the tribe.

Many an evening I'd stay for dinner and had fun making little packets of knives and forks and spoons all individually bandaged up in paper napkins for the Douglases. Then we'd take up our plates with salad and beef stroganoff on them and the packets and go into the TV room and watch Lloyd Bridges in *Seahunt* and the evening news with Huntley and Brinkley. Oftentimes Mr. Douglas or one of the boys would not be home but it sure beat waiting until eight o'clock when my dad got home.

I can remember Tracy and my comparing Huntley to Brinkley. She said that Huntley brought out the father image and Brinkley brought out the little boy image. She liked Brinkley. I liked Huntley. This was about all we got out of the news at this time except for Eisenhower playing golf.

Back in biology class, we did the old story of "The Birds and the Bees" and how the flowers get pollinated and fertilized. I noticed many of the class members really went into a fast act when Miss Fair would talk about the pistil and the ovary. I was still drawing parts of a typical flower as though they were designs in coloring books but when I think of it, those drawings taught me that I didn't know what I could do until I tried.

Late in the first semester, we learned about molds, mushrooms and algae and finally dissected an earthworm. Of course, the specimens were kept in formaldehyde jars and it was a little bit hard getting into the visible and nonvisible structure—not using and using the microscope.

I had a very interesting end to the first semester of biology. We had live specimens and I learned that the earthworm has a nervous system that reacts to certain stimuli just as people do. Sound interesting? I only got a check on my report—seems that I left out the conclusion: "that all living things depend to some degree on other forms of life."

Well, I never knew an explorer who did it all by himself. I always believed that there had to be someone to check out the facts. Hence, what I thought was obvious, the conclusion that was missing from my lab manual that first semester, resulted in my getting just an average grade from Miss Fair. She gave me a C minus. I was bucking for a B minus, coloring book of flowers and all. I was beginning to think she was anything but fair.

During the winter vacation and semester break, I was frequently at Tracy's house. The Douglases were enthusiastic people and on rainy days when Tracy and I didn't play records (our favorite was the Kingston Trio album), we'd play jacks on the kitchen floor or bridge with Tracy's brothers and her mother. Her older brother, Ray, was home from Hamilton College and in the midst of transferring to the University of California at Berkeley. Dick, her younger brother, was a senior at Menlo High School. He must have been part boy scout as he never let the fire in the fireplace dwindle. He always added another log. I was attracted to Ray and he knew it. But he remained more interested in his cards than in me and played a good game of bridge.

Sometimes, with the help of Mrs. Douglas, I learned some of what the game was all about. She stood over me like a mother hen and told me what cards to play and why. I had never had advice like this from anyone. I thought it was just a game.

The spring semester in biology spun right along with the dissection of a fish, a frog and, finally, with the study of human anatomy's framework and function. I discovered a fish had teeth, a frog had a brain and a human being had a four-chambered heart among other similar organs or singular differences.

Miss Fair was impressed with my improved handwritten reports but would only give me a check, not a check mark with a plus because they were usually one or two days late. She would write the check plus and then add the criticism, "late"; hence the check mark underlined. It was almost impossible for me to do the kind of work she estimated as being in a B student's capacity, as she not only wanted the best drawings, correct labelings and legibly written lab reports, she wanted them turned into her fast. I think the only A grade she gave was to herself for being able to correct all the class papers—fast.

Before the spring vacation, Miss Fair announced that each of the nine students in my Biology 10 class would be expected to do a Final Project and that it would count one-third of her grade for the year. I was horrified. I was doing okay in the second semester, averaging a C, but now if I didn't do a good job on this project, I could see that grade being threatened.

I remained after class and asked Miss Fair what would be a good final project for me to do. She looked at me and said that *I* should think about it and by the end of the week, tell her what I had chosen. This left me in about as vague a state as when I approached her to ask my question.

After the next few days, I still didn't have any ideas. I stayed after class again and told her that I didn't know what to do for my final project. Miss Fair got up from her desk, moved to one of the student tables, sat on it and said that there could be a lot of things to do and that I should enlarge on some of the ideas presented in class. I looked blank.

She added that there were some things she could suggest that hadn't already been chosen by other students. She told me that I could do two posters of flowers showing them in their dormant period and their blooming period. "Uh-huh," I thought, "more coloring book pictures of flowers—no thanks!"

She saw that I wasn't going for that idea so she said that another thought was to take some little plants, put them in a closet for a couple of weeks and take photos of them every so often to show how they don't do well without light. Uh-huh, the old photosynthesis principle again—no thanks.

Miss Fair said that those were about all she could suggest unless I wanted to do a paper on a scientific subject such as the International Geophysical Year. I remember saying, "A paper! I could do a paper. A report?"

She said, "Yes."

At last I had selected my final project.

I then asked her what the International Geophysical Year was and she smiled and said, "You find out and you tell me in your paper." I asked her how long she'd like it to be and she said whatever I thought was necessary to do the assignment.

Around April, my parents and the Hewitts, some good friends of theirs, were going to New York for a combined business and pleasure trip. I was going to stay at the Hewitts in San Mateo during that time. Mrs. Hewitt had her Aunt Martha staying at her white brick house on Chester Way so that the everyday household routine would not be interrupted and I would get to know their sons, Howard and little Jimmy. Howard was a junior in high school, close to six feet tall and had a car. Jimmy was in elementary school and had his own friends.

In the evening after we all had dinner, Aunt Martha helped Jimmy with his homework. Howard and I snacked together on Aunt Martha's Eagle Brand cookies and played Monopoly together in the den. We went for rides in the early evening's springness in his MG, going to the library to do our school work or just driving around.

Towards the end of my stay, we went out to a couple of movies. stopped at the local A & W drive-in restaurant for root beers and headed up the hill to see the night time views and make doughnuts in the fields.

At the end of the ten day stay, I had an invitation to the Corte Madera Military School's Spring Prom and Howard had an invitation to The Orchard's Spring Ball. We weren't exactly "going with each other" but we had found each other...with the help of our parents. It was a comfortable relationship with chemistry that was all our own.

When I got back to Atherton after my parents' return, I had Spring Fever. If I wasn't on the phone talking to Howard, I was over at Tracy's talking about Howard—how great he was and how much fun he was. She replied with as many positive and affirmative responses she could think of and then finally asked me if I thought I could get Howard to fix her up with one of his friends so we could both go to the proms. I remember saying, "I'll try."

How do you describe a chubby, well, more than just chubby—downright heavy-with-fat girlfriend who could make anyone laugh just by putting a sweater on? How do you tell your boyfriend you want him to find a friend of his to take your friend to the dance? You say, "She has a great personality and he won't be sorry that he took her out." Right? Meanwhile, Tracy is thinking that she is going to get stuck with a clod (a non-plus personality) but because it's a momentous occasion, maybe she can make the most of it.

Howard came through and arranged it so that Claude would take Tracy to the Spring Ball. I could hardly bring myself to tell Tracy that her fears of getting stuck with a clod only amounted to her getting stuck with a Claude and that it would be fun because at least we would be double-dating and in the same car...Claude's—the original high school heap! What more of a sacrifice could Tracy expect of me? If it wasn't for doubling, I could be going in Howard's sports car. However, this way Howard and I did have the back seat to ourselves.

The day of the date came and when Tracy met Claude and saw the dandruff on the collar and shoulders of his suit, I know she could have socked me one in the tum-tum. I just smiled and said, "Let's hurry along or we'll be late and miss the rock and roll before they begin *Blue Moon.*

It all worked out. Although Claude found Tracy's weight problem more than he was ready for, he was able to chit-chat and Tracy could banter back. We did have a few laughs that night and more the next day.

After my heavy social season, I realized I had only two weeks left to discover what the International Geophysical Year was all about. I spent the entire Saturday of the first weekend in the largest library nearby, Redwood City. I had my mother drop me off at 10:00 am and told her not to come back until 3:00 to pick me up. I was on an assignment trip.

The first thing I learned was that the IGY ran between July 1, 1957 and December 31, 1958 and involved over forty nations. With footnoted facts such as the technical planning of the program on a worldwide basis was accomplished through a series of meetings of various international committees, it appeared to be a very unspecific program to describe. I was looking up information in references that I had never before become acquainted with: *The National Science Foundation 6th Annual Report, 1956, Science News Letter*, and various science service publications. The first trip to the library was a disappointment to me because I realized that all of the information I needed came out of periodicals which were only in the library. I couldn't work on the project at home.

However, I did discover that since my mother was a collector of periodicals herself, preferably fashion magazines, *Time* and newspapers, that I could search through the stacked papers in the garage. With luck I'd find pictures and articles to cut out that would enhance my report. I found pictures on Project Vanguard, the artifical earth satellite which was not a success; there was an explosion on the blast-off. Also, an article that at Cape Canaveral, Florida, on December 6, 1957, a three and one-fourth pound ball, still emitting its tracking voice despite damage, was found and that President Eisenhower was disappointed in its inability to get off the ground.

The next Saturday I also spent in serious library research and made copious notes. It seemed that the most successful part of the IGY was the U. S. program on Operation Deepfreeze, the Antarctic Expedition of Admiral Richard E. Byrd. I had gathered my notes, my resources and was ready with a decorated cover and bibliography to write my paper for Miss Fair.

The paper amounted to seven typed pages plus pictures and a cover that showed a cartoon from *The New Yorker*. The picture was of five African witch doctors sitting inside a hut. The caption read: "Let's reveal the location of the hidden volcano as our contribution to the Geophysical Year." I have a sense of humor and I felt this report was so far out that it needed a good laugh. I still have the cartoon in a scrap book.

Miss Fair accepted my report, handed in two days late, and thanked me. I sure felt that I had done a hell of a good job. I went up and down those stairs at The Orchard like I was some kind of whiz kid. I was guessing at my grade. I thought an A minus, then I thought a B plus. I had no idea that when the final grades were announced that I would receive an F.

"I don't understand," I said and I repeated myself... saying the same thing over and over until Miss Fair broke in and said,

"Your report was late. I had to penalize you because of the late work. I had originally given you a D."

I said, "A D! Do you know how much work I put into this paper!"

She said that she knew I had done research on the subject but that there were too many footnotes and not enough of my own words.

My own words! How do you describe geomagnetism, ionospheric physics, cosmic rays and upper atmospheric rocket activity in your own words? I was speechless. I couldn't believe anyone would give out an F on a final project. Yet, it had been my secret fear all along that this would happen.

I asked her if she liked the cartoon on the cover and she replied that she didn't think it had anything to do with the assignment. I felt sick and angry and didn't know what I could do. I pulled myself together, though, and asked her, "How does this affect my final grade for the course?"

Miss Fair looked at her grade book, flipping a couple of pages, and said, "Your final grade point comes to a 69."

I asked her, "What is that?" (knowing it was a D). She confirmed the fact that the year's grade point would be a D. I felt both very angry and very sorry for this unmerciful creature.

I looked at her and she looked at me and said, "See, average it out for yourself. I did it twice and it comes out 69."

I thought, "Gee! Thanks! How kind of you to take the time!"

My thoughts then turned towards how my parents were going to accept this "good news." I said, "Do you know that with grades like this that my parents will not be spending money to send me to this private school, if all I can bring home are D's?"

She just said, "I'm sorry; your work was late!"

Well, kiss Wellesley good-bye and the rest of the seven sister colleges. I now knew where I wasn't going to go to college but I wasn't sure where I *was* going to go. I had to do better but I was beginning to wonder why, as grades seemed to be a game of chance and as long as Miss Fair turned out to be Miss Fink, why bother? My pride had been hurt and my brain crossed.

Chrysanthemums in Bloom

He is not alive anymore. He died before he was forty-five but he taught European history, Asian history and current history at The Orchard while I was there. I took every one of his courses. He taught his classes without a textbook.

Ronald Rickles believed that one had to learn to take notes from lectures and the better you took them, the better the chances you had of passing his weekly quizzes. The outside reports accompanying the periods being studied were to be chosen from a book list that he compiled of classic, historical novels, biographies and best sellers. The reports were never expected to be over five hundred words. He didn't expect miracles; he just wanted to teach history so it would inspire responses from his students and they would retain some knowledge of what civilization was all about.

Mr. Rickles was tall and had wiry, waving hair which he cut very short. He wore a tie, slacks and sports coat and was never very animated. He would lecture from his notes, pause, and look up at the class for a time and then go into a personal recollection or a joke. He had traveled all over the world. (His parents had been missionaries in China.) He would pause so that the class wouldn't take notes on his jokes but some were so good...I'm sorry that I didn't. They usually focused on a social, economic or political insight that pointed out hypocrisy.

My junior year I took European history. The classroom was on the third floor and I sat closest to the door in the front row. There were about twenty-four students from other classes in the upper school. This was one of the largest classes except for P. E. I think I sat near the door so that I could get in and out of the classroom quickly. As I remember, recess followed and I smoked.

Tracy Douglas had left The Orchard this year for Menlo High School but the herd that puffed on cigarettes was still around. We certainly had mixed feelings when our favorite smoking area had been progressively trimmed down and then entirely removed. The echoes of *Hang Down Your Head Tom Dooley* seemed to linger over the bare ground.

The grove had disappeared and there was only one thing to do...break up the group...we had been discovered! Besides, some of the members were driving cars and it became easier to just park your car down the road and then go off campus for lunch, cokes and cigarettes.

I still liked my seat next to the door in Mr. Rickles' class even though the recess break had lost some of its importance. It was just that it seemed like an independent seat and, of course, no one took down his words as well as I did or enjoyed his jokes as much. I wonder what a psychologist would say about liking my end row seat as I kept the same position as my choice for all his classes. I had also chosen my major for college, naturally, history.

There was another girl, new, a transfer, who also laughed at Mr. Rickles' jokes and who asked him questions to make him further expand on his recollections. I thought she had a nice, outgoing personality. Her name was Beth Moore.

Since recess had become milk and cookie time again, I thought I would be gregarious and find out where Beth lived and what she liked to do. She seemed studious since she didn't stand around the tables and chit-chat in the dining room. Instead she sat on a couch in the main hallway reading an assignment notebook and making additional notes in it, while sipping through a straw stuck in a half-pint milk carton. I approached her and asked if she had a minute.

Beth looked up, smiled, squinted her eyes and then flashed them. "Sure."

"This is your first year here at The Orchard and I wondered where you live."

"Hillview," she replied quickly.

I then asked her where she had transferred from. Once again came a fast reply, "Montebello."

I knew that Montebello was a girls' boarding school and one of the few in California that allowed you to have your own horse on the school grounds. Showing off my knowledge of what Montebello was all about, I followed with my next question.

"Did you like boarding school and do you like to ride horses?"

Beth just sort of ignored the first part of the question. She said that she had been away from Hillview for her first two years of high school and that she liked being home with her sisters and brothers and that her hobby was equestrian riding.

In the middle of my quest of finding out what she liked to do, she got up from the couch, piled up her binder and books and looked towards the stairs that go up to the second floor.

I walked with her, departed to fetch my books and returned huffing, to catch up with her on the landing of the second floor. I asked her where she did her horseback riding.

She sort of mumbled the name of some stables in Hillview then started walking towards a classroom. Following in her steps, I asked her if she had her own horse. She stopped, gave me a clear, piercing look and said, "I have two."

I thought, "Wow! That's neat!" She could take someone riding with her. I ventured to recite my English riding experiences but she interrupted with another concise look and said, "Why don't you try to find a friend down in Atherton?"

Flattened, punctured, hurt and wondering what I had done wrong, I wasn't going to let flickering eyes and a gracious smile ever again make me feel so small. It seemed to me that Beth Moore didn't need pets, people or Santa Claus. She was a one-piece marching band.

As I watched her more, I saw the first straight A student in my junior class. She would continue her straight A average in her senior year and be elected Student Body President of The Orchard's Upper School, solidly on the ladder to success.

It wasn't that I never saw an A; I did. I was a straight A student in French 2A. Of course, it was the second time I took it. I liked French. There was a difference of opinion about what sophomore year French was all about between me and Madame Rene. I received a recommendation to take it over before progressing...that a repetition of the course would strengthen my language elective course background. I wasn't upset, just glad to be out of that person's class and into a comparatively easier class. My grades in French went: French 1A, an A (refresher from when I had French at another school), then French 2A, a D. (One didn't do written exercises; one was supposed to recite poetry on tapes in the language lab.)

Now I was doing one hundred percent again with French 2A because the teacher liked us to read from our prepared written exercises. This different approach to the same course taught me that it wasn't the course number that was important but the instructor. I didn't want to go to French 3A with Madame Rene anymore than she wanted me there. It was mutual.

But Madame Figorette made me an A student because I always double checked my French exercises and read the textbook stories well in class. I'm afraid that today my French conversation is not very good but I know a few of the words on a French menu and I can pronounce "Chanel."

While Beth Moore had beheaded me, she had given me an idea. There was a girl in my French 2A class who never had her exercises completed and would hand in an assignment two-thirds finished. Her name was Judy Christopher. I recognized her riding on the school bus and at school but never really got to know her. She got off the school bus at one of the mass unloading stops at Lakeside. There was a country store on the corner where the bus stopped and sometimes the students riding on farther down to Atherton would get out and buy gum or an ice-cream bar while the bus waited.

I had learned much from Beth. I figured that if I sat in the front of the bus and double checked my French exercises and looked busy, maybe Judy would join me and get her French exercises finished on the bus ride to The Orchard.

Judy Christopher had been at The Orchard as long as I had. We had that in common. We also would have French in common if she wanted me to go over her homework with her. Judy had many friends at Lakeside High School and seemed to have more going for her on the outside than at school. She was also independent enough to get babysitting jobs, something that I tried once. At 11:00 pm my father came to the house where I was babysitting and sent me home with my mother while he stayed until one in the morning. Needless to say, I didn't get rehired and I didn't go looking for anymore babysitting jobs. Financially, I was definitely a dependent. Judy was very practical but light-hearted...she knew what she was good at and knew what she wasn't keen in. French 2A was beginning to become a problem for her.

For another few days I was still shuffling my French (typed) exercises back and forth on the school bus and flashing a gigantic French dictionary up and down in the air on to and off of my stack of books. Finally, after French 2A class, I stared at Judy, caught her eye for a few seconds and then found myself at her desk.

"You don't like this class very much do you?"

Judy said, "I don't do very well in any foreign language. I like math."

I said, "Well, sometimes it takes two to get the exercises checked over. I don't like math and always need those problems checked over."

I said that I would be happy to help her with the French exercises on the morning school bus ride if she would sit next to me. I'd save her a seat.

She agreed and said that she had thought of asking me a few times on the bus but didn't have the courage. She didn't want to cheat or copy...just get the class over with.

We left that classroom like two long lost survivors of the Civil War and on the same side. Judy had a friend in our class year whom she wanted to have lunch with and introduce me to. Now the test of whether to run out to the secret, hidden car for a cigarette escape or to stay with Judy and meet her friend (who might be dull). It was a challenge. I thought, "Well, Judy knows that I smoke; she saw cigarettes in my purse. If she can put up with me, I can forget the cigarette run."

Judy introduced me to Betty Dowd and told Betty how smart I was in French. (I wish she had played that down.) Also, that I lived in Atherton. I knew who Betty was but didn't know her well. Suddenly, it all jelled. We all took European history together! Betty Dowd wanted me to meet her friend Rosalie Marchand, also in our class but newly transferred. At lunch, everyone was usually so busy eating fast that there wasn't time for super-intellectual conversation. However, Betty Dowd showed her colors by telling us that she and Rosalie were going to make millions on a beaver fur bikini. "My gosh, why not?" I thought.

Rosalie Marchand looked at me and said, "You're the one who laughs out loud at Mr. Rickles' jokes."

I said, "Yes, but I'm not the only one; there is one other."

Rosalie didn't say anything more. It appeared that she wasn't one to cause controversy but to go along with the general swing of things and yet she had a lightning streak in her to come up with beaver fur bikinis.

The European history class was growing closer or farther apart. There were the students in favor of Mr. Rickles and the ones who were just taking the course for credit. After winter finals, it was proposed that those who wished to sign up for a dinner at *La Maison Rouge, Blanc et Bleu* do so, with preambles at Mr. Ronald Rickles' apartment in San Francisco.

Only twelve students signed up. As usual, not everyone was interested but out of the twelve were my new-found friends, Judy Christopher, Betty Dowd and Rosalie Marchand. There was to be an individual fee of six dollars for the dinner and tip. The dinner included a butter lettuce salad, broiled lamb chops and legumes (green beans, no doubt) and a Napoleon for dessert.

Rosalie drove her station wagon and had Betty, Judy and me meet her at her house in Hillview. I drove my family's newly purchased Dodge Lancer 500 and picked up Judy at her home in Lakeside. It was the first time Judy had seen a car with push button automatic transmission. She liked the style and mentioned how comfortable the seat was. When we all got organized and packed into Rosalie's wagon, we were filled with anticipation. We were going to see Mr. Rickles' apartment.

"Too bad he wasn't going to the dinner, too!" we said.

Rosalie really maneuvered that huge station wagon around the city avenues and streets. We got to Mr. Rickles' street and near his address block and Rosalie said, "Isn't that Ron Rickles?" We looked out the windows and in no time, agreed.

She stopped her car at the crosswalk and blinked her headlights, high, low, low, high. Mr. Rickles had been identified. He came over to the car and looked in Rosalie's door window.

"Hi. You can park wherever you can find a place. Just don't block any of the driveways," he said.

We all giggled, knowing we had found our first destination point.

As she pressed her foot on the gas pedal, Rosalie said, "Did you notice he was carrying a little brown paper bag? I bet it was from the liquor store on the corner."

I was shocked. How did Rosalie pick up that bit of information! It could have been candy bars from the market also on the corner.

Parked, we all strolled towards Mr. Rickles' apartment. We were the first to arrive. I always think that shows who really cares. Anyway, we were the first and this also gave us more time for scrutinizing.

Mr. Rickles, dressed informally in a turtle neck and slacks, opened the door. I thought that *that* was mighty new. He seemed very much at ease. Somehow, I had the feeling that this was his night. He didn't hesitate to show us to his bedroom and ask us to leave our wraps and coats on his bed. I looked at the bed and thought, "King Size! Well, all kings should have a lot of room!"

We were a little at loss for words when Judy piped up and asked if he shared the apartment. He said that he had two roommates. Then we moved into the "free-style room". It would be called a lanai if it were in a house on the peninsula. It was the size of a studio but there were no library shelves, hence, an entertaining room—not large, not tight, just right.

Mr. Rickles had some mixed nuts for us to munch on and some pretzels and asked us if we would like a 7 Up. There was a hi-fi with its speakers turned on but I can't remember the music. We were beginning to enjoy our "Big Night in Frisco". Rosalie nudged me while I was eating one half of the mixed nuts and said, "Do you know there are only two separate bedrooms here?"

"So?" I said.

She looked at me and said that he had two roommates, emphasizing the "two".

I said, "Well, maybe one sleeps on the couch in the living room." What was she making such a big deal out of? Rosalie was surprising.

Meanwhile, when I went back to the mixed nuts, Mr. Rickles was having a 7 Up which some of us had accepted and some hadn't. I can't remember too much except those nuts and that he said to me, "Do you like to go to different places?"

I said, "Sure, I like to go out."

He then dipped into his fish bowl filled with match books from different restaurants and pulled one out with a nude female on it. It said in flaming red letters, *The Dice Club.* I said that I had never been there. He handed it to me very slowly, with the greatest amount of tenderness, his hand lingering on mine. I can still feel the sensuality of his touch today.

By the time all concerned had arrived at the apartment, we were ready to leave. As we picked up our wraps and coats, I took a second look at Mr. Rickles' bed. No doubt he had more "City Women" than he knew what to do with. Living in "The City" with all the great places to go became a definite goal.

Rosalie found the restaurant with no trouble. Our group in the station wagon was quiet all but for Judy describing the pictures on the walls at Rickles' apartment. "Did you notice the abstracts?" she'd say. No one came up with any response. Even Rosalie was quiet but then she was driving. Maybe some, like me, were trying to keep the event to ourselves to protect the memory.

La Maison Rouge, Blanc et Bleu was small. The banquet room was in the back and was arranged for twelve places. So far the only unique thing had been the waiters in their black tuxes and the red and white table cloths with the blue linen napkins.

The salad was served and then a new face appeared at the doorway with a large key around his neck. He asked us if we wanted to have any wine served with our dinner. I looked at him and feeling all of twenty-eight, said, "Yes, I think so," looking at Betty Dowd who smiled at me. I was prepared to pay for the wine myself if I had to.

I said, "We would like some vin rose, s'il vous plait."

He bowed. I don't remember if he clicked his heels but he was very debonaire and we all had a glass of rose wine to celebrate the evening. I think that sort of touched off the evening for me. I was taking responsibility for the group, with courage, and the group did not turn me down. However, I was not very verbose, thinking only of the total evening. Betty's look when I ordered the wine was one of amazement and I felt that she really saw me for the first time in three years.

Late in the spring quarter my social life developed unexpectedly. Judy Christopher, who was copying my French exercises every day on the morning bus ride, would get involved in matchmaking in the afternoon. She would tell me she knew this neat guy from Lakeside High School who didn't have a steady. I'd laugh and say, "He really must be a winner."

She kept telling me how neat Gene Keller was and could she give him my telephone number?

I'd listen and say, "Why would he want to meet me?"

She'd say that he'd heard her talk of me and he really wanted to meet me. She thought it would really be good for both of us to talk to each other.

I said, "Sure. Give him my phone number but just because he's six feet and two inches and handsome and works on his car doesn't impress me because I know a friend of the family who is very steady for special occasions.

Judy jumped right in on the special occasions and said, "Who are you taking to the April Charity Ball?"

I said, "I haven't given it much thought, but probably Howard Hewitt."

She said, "No, don't think about Howard. Think about your new challenge, Gene Keller."

I was razzle-dazzled. Gene called me; told me how many times he had seen me.

I said, "Where?"

He said, "At the bus stop at Lakeside."

I *was* impressed.

We had a couple of cozy dates at his home. I met his parents, saw his small room and listened to him play the trumpet. He met my parents and I saw to it that we didn't stick around for too much socializing. (My mother has the habit of finding out if everyone I bring into the house is a Democrat or a Republican.) I just wanted to get into his high school heap and watch the sun set with him.

Judy was right. Gene and I were a perfect match. We couldn't spend forty-eight hours away from each other without a telephone call or a date. I remember one rather imbecilic telephone conversation that had us arguing over the potential of liking or disliking peas. He hated peas and I said, "But they are so colorful with carrots." I was not a good promoter as far as vegetables went.

The spring Charity Ball came up on the calendar and I invited Gene. I also made it clear that the theme was Hawaiian and that instead of a single flower, a Hawaiian lei would be nice with my strapless formal. Well, it seemed to me that it was as important to have a lei at a Hawaiian formal dance as it is for some women to have a chrysanthemum corsage when they go to the annual Big Game between Stanford and California.

I lived to regret that hint when I found out that carnation leis ran fifteen dollars and that was almost his total weekly pay from working at the hardware store part time. Why he bothered with me until we parted during my senior year, I'll never know. I think he liked the prestige of dating a "private school girl." I'd marry him tomorrow but today I have no place in his life.

He lives in Hawaii and flies his own plane and is saved from having me spend all of his money. He was a million dollar crush for me. This chapter doesn't really end because I can say that about fifteen other guys but there really isn't anything like doing things the first time...like Charity Balls.

Pressed Rose Petals

What a potpourri of prismatic events I recall leading
me on, and beyond, my pristine age. Between my junior and
senior year, I was fortunate enough to travel to Europe on a
select girl's tour that originated from San Francisco. There
were only ten girls, six from San Francisco, three from Marin
County and me from the Peninsula. Also, I was the only one
under eighteen years of age, the rest having graduated from
high school and going abroad for five weeks before they
started college or art school.

Some of the girls had even been to Europe before and
would say that such and such was different from when they
were there in '57. I was among post debutantes and very
wealthy bankers' daughters but with my background of European history from The Orchard, I did not feel unequal.

I sat on the Volkswagon bus with the three girls from
Marin County. Our chaperone, Miss Stacey, was an art history teacher at Lowell High School in San Francisco. She
marched us in and out of churches and museums so fast that
we nicknamed her Racey Stacey but she was just the oppo-

site of that at the luncheon and dining places along the tour. She took her time, enjoyed the wine that flowed with the meals...day in...day out...and we did too.

I also found out that if one wanted to go down to a hotel lounge in Paris, Rome or out into St. Mark's Square in Venice, that one could order, from the bar or a sidewalk cafe, an aperitif or a martini. The waiter sometimes didn't look any older than I was or, sometimes, he was so old he could have been my grandfather but they never asked for any age identification.

I was getting good at drinking martinis even though the first one in Rome was a bit bitter. I asked the waiter who understood a little English (after all, we were on the Via Veneto) why the martini tasted so bitter.

"Ah," he said. "You *do* not like our Italian gin?"

"Italian gin?" I said.

"Si," he replied. Then he asked me if I would rather have a martini made with English gin.

I thought for a moment. That's right! English gin, of course! I said, "Yes, please, take this Italian martini away." I had just won a free game on the pinball machine. Wait until I tell the girls from Marin County about my discovery!

I enjoyed the tour: the trip from New York City to Le Havre on the United States Lines to Paris and the picnics and wine tasting in the Loire Valley and the other cities visited...Munich, Germany, Velden in Austria and most of Italy including the Amalfi Drive, Sorrento and Capri with stopovers in Switzerland and the trip back to Paris before going over to England and seeing London and Shakespeare country.

I was different from the girls on the tour. I had a boyfriend waiting for me in California so I opted to fly home instead of taking the ship. My flight reservation was on a prop plane and it took twenty-two hours with a stopover for gas in Newfoundland. One week later it was announced that transcontinental jets would be replacing propeller planes on all overseas flights, July 1959.

Of course, I had a reason for returning five days early. I had Gene. He was working full time at the hardware store during the summer. I telephoned him at his house in the evening soon after I got home and after making sure I had privacy (closing the door in the master bedroom while the folks were in the den at the opposite end of the house), I dialed his number.

His mother answered, naturally, and I announced who I was. She was happy to call Gene to the phone. After what seemed like five years instead of five weeks, I was talking to Gene.

"Thanks for all those letters on that tissue paper stationery," he said.

He sort of coughed and muttered something about how I probably should have partied more. I felt a twinge. I didn't understand what he meant. We paused and then I said, "I brought you a souvenir."

He said, "When can I see you?"

I said, "I'm not doing anything Friday night."

He said, "Friday night looks fine. I'd like to take you to the *Spaghetti Factory* in San Francisco for dinner."

"Oh, that would be neat!" Did you know that there are two kinds of spaghetti—red and green?"

"I guess so," he said. "How about six o'clock, ready or not?"

I said, "I'll be ready."

So the summer of 1959 came to an end and I had progressed to having been abroad with a diletante's exposure of having seen some of the greatest art in the world. However, it didn't really change me except for giving me knowledge and respect for the Vatican and for taking a genuine interest in and liking for Pope John XXIII. He had spoken to a huge audience in St. Peter's the Wednesday afternoon that I was there and said that if they really wanted peace, they would have to pray for it. I didn't understand this philosophy at the time but the older I get, I can see more truth than fallacy in it. Meanwhile, going into my last year at The Orchard, I was still hoping to make good grades.

There had been a change at The Orchard, Miss DiSalvo had been replaced by Mrs. Hitchcock as Headmistress. Miss DiSalvo, who had tried to treat all of the school's pupils as equals with a ready ear for their problems, had resigned. Some parents had thought that her casualness was not effective and that she would be better with older, college level students needing discipline. So we had a Mrs. Hitchcock.

Mrs. Hitchcock was an obvious executive. She was terribly bright—always with a word or with an action and she had one daughter who was enrolled at The Orchard. Mrs. Hitchcock held credentials of the uppermost from the University of California, including a Ph.D. in Education and she specialized in the exceptional child. She was a new rhythm in the band.

I came back to school and looked at the Academic Calendar posted on the bulletin board in the main downstairs hallway. It read: Oct. 14: Preliminary Scholastic Aptitude Tests (Juniors). (Well, I had had mine last year, including sitting in a seat under a burnt out bulb in the light fixture at History Corner at Stanford and when the director of the test, wearing a hearing aid, asked if there were any questions, I said, "Yes, I can't see." He didn't hear me and the test started.)

Also on the calendar was the date Nov. 4: CEEB Scholastic Aptitude Tests (Seniors) Special Date. (I wondered what that was for. I had this feeling I was in a brain factory.) Then on the calendar was Dec. 2: CEEB Scholastic Aptitude Tests (Seniors). Then, Dec. 13: Term Examinations and Dec. 14: Christmas Program and Holiday Begins. (Thank goodness.)

The calendar continued, January 2: 8:30 School Re-opens. (All good things must come to an end.)

Then in big letters: Second Term—and it was every bit as bad as the first.

I'm not even going to try to list the rest of the Advanced Placement Tests and Senior Final Examinations because it is all so much the pattern of all highly academic schools and that is just what Mrs. Hitchcock was determined to mold The Orchard into. There was, finally, at some future magic date, the Commencement Rehearsal and Commencement.

More power to Mrs. Hitchcock but she was not of my era. I belonged to the loose, left-footed ways of doing things until I found out myself that there was a right-footed way of doing things—on my own—without a brain scan. However, she was helpful. She saw to it that there were more faculty meetings and seemed to cultivate an image that The Orchard was growing and was going to be the best. I admired her for this. But I was on my way out. I would miss the total centrifugation.

I had really anticipated no run-ins with Mrs. Hitchcock. However, never say *never*.

I was still a tribe member of the Douglases and we all remembered each other with gifts at Christmas time. Tracy Douglas had gone on to making new friends at Menlo High School and I met her closest friend, Clarissa, and we all laughed at Jonathan Winters and Shelley Berman records, listening to them on the hi-fi.

Tracy was my ready ear for the tale of how Gene Keller had "sort of" dropped me after Thanksgiving. Also in on this saga was Tracy's brother, Ray, who was often home from Cal on the weekends and who pretty well knew most of what was going on with "the girls".

Christmas time came. On the twenty-third I dropped by 222 Greenoaks with my presents and stayed to open mine. Mrs. Douglas gave me a darling cashmere cardigan, white with little patches of color on it. Tracy gave me a record album, *Mr. Lucky,* by Henry Mancini. Dick didn't give me anything but Ray gave me this dear little half-pint flask that was sterling silver or something like it with the words *Little Nipper* engraved on it. It was from Abercrombie and Fitch. He said that it should be good for an hour class. When I was in college, I got the drift of what he meant but I didn't exactly understand then. Anyway, I was delighted.

I said, "We should fill it up."

Ray said, "We will;" but we didn't then.

Now that I was a free woman and not dating Gene Keller, I was looking at Ray Douglas with a different 'scope. He was eligible, over twenty-one, taking courses at Cal and attractively intellectual-looking with glasses and slightly thinning hair. He was not a high schooler with part time work at a hardware store and he drove a car that did not require spending the total week-end tuning it up. Anyway, there was going to be this dance at Beth Moore's house in Hillview. I wasn't "too big" on going but I thought if I invited Ray maybe I'd have a good time.

I waited until Ray was home on a week-end and asked him if he would like to go to a St. Patrick's Day Dance in Hillview at Beth Moore's.

He said, "Who is Beth Moore?"

That made my day! I said, "Well, she is this terribly

wealthy girl and has a neat house in Hillview." I also added, "You may not get another chance to see such a really, genuine Hillview mansion."

"I'll go," Ray said.

But, the way he said it made me feel my sales campaign had gone past me.

Anyway, we went. I had brought my little flask along with me and after Ray picked me up, I asked him if we could fill it up. We stopped at Menlo Park's elite liquor store and transferred part of the bottle into the half pint flask, storing the left-over gin under the driver's seat.

I said, "This is going to be fun!"

Ray said, "Why not!"

When we got to Beth's in Hillview, we were impressed but not too "ah'ed." Her house was just big with a big stairway that went to the second floor. It was evident that there was a large family living there. The difference between Beth and me was that I lived like Cinderella while she had sisters and brothers and never had to worry about anything except her schoolwork and exercising her horses because they had household help.

Ray and I were shown the dancing area. The living room had all its rugs pulled back and the furniture pushed back to the walls. Beth's cousin, Lee, had set up the new stereo apparatus with separate speakers. I looked at Ray and he looked at me and we danced for about fifteen minutes to *S'Wonderful, S'Marvelous,* a Ray Coniff tape.

Then Ray said that he was thirsty. I agreed and we looked around for the punch bowl. It was too early yet. We spent time talking to Lee. He was sort of the engineer type and had set up the amplification system. Ray was getting tired of talking about tweeters and looked at me.

"Why don't we just have a cold 7 Up from the ice

chest?" I said.

Ray said, "Fine."

While we were drinking our 7 Ups, I said to Ray, "When do you think we should spike the punch?"

Ray looked at me and said, "You Devil, you!"

I said, "I wasn't born yesterday; I've been to Europe, you know!"

Ray said, "I knew there was something that I liked about you, kid."

As the rest of the expected couples had arrived, Beth announced that the punch was ready.

Ray now had the flask, *Little Nipper*, in the inside pocket of his sports coat.

I said, "Let's not get caught!"

Ray said, "No problem, my dear. You just stand to my right while I empty *Little Nipper* into the punch bowl." He did exactly that!

I took the empty flask and put it into my purse with my coat in the coat room. We were conspirators.

The punch was delightful. We had seconds...and danced for an hour to the melodies of *So Rare, Somewhere Beyond the Sea* and *Smoke Gets in your Eyes*.

It was about 11:30 and there had been certain rumblings about the punch having been spiked and a new batch had appeared.

Ray and I didn't encore. We were ready to leave.

I went to get my coat and purse and met him in the foyer. We left, smiling and saying good nights.

It wasn't until I was in the car that I looked inside my purse and my coat pocket and couldn't come up with *Little Nipper.*

Ray said, "What do you mean, you can't find it?"

I said that they had taken *Little Nipper* out of my

purse and I was probably going to be in deep water Monday morning.

Ray just replied, "Don't worry; you weren't on school grounds."

I said, "Beth Moore's is about as close to school grounds as you can get !"

Ray just said, "Don't worry."

And I didn't...not then...on the way home that night.

On Monday morning I rode the bus. No one was driving to school anymore unless she was a senior. As Mrs. Hitchcock put it, "It is a senior privilege to be allowed to drive on Fridays only and to park your cars on the school grounds since the town of Hillview has requested that students' cars are not to be parked on the residential streets around the school."

As the bus ride picked up momentum, I thought to myself, "What if the flask just disappeared and I'd never see it again? No one will say anything about it." I liked that idea. My stomach felt better and I was less tense. When we got to Lakeside, Judy got on the bus and I handed her my French homework as usual. Nothing different from the routine so far. We even talked a little bit about the dance. Judy hadn't gone. I assured her she hadn't missed a thing.

The school day progressed. I was sure that the disappearance of *Little Nipper* was going to be forgotten when around 2:30 I was tapped out of P. E. and asked to change my clothes and see Mrs. Hitchcock.

I knew she knew. However, I also knew that I wasn't Miss Perfect and that my biggest mistake was putting the flask in my purse instead of just letting Ray hang on to it until we got in the car.

What could I say? Well, Mrs. Hitchcock, it's not the first time that someone under twenty-one has had a drink.

Then I thought about my parents finding out. That was worse than anything Mrs. Hitchcock could do to me. Their scolding and seeing to it that I wore sackcloth to reduce my ego to the size of a pinhead was something I could never get used to. I could hear them both now. You never do anything right. I don't know how a child of mine could be so dumb.

Well, maybe Mrs. Hitchcock would be bon-bons compared to my imagining. Maybe she and I could have this little conference without my parents finding out.

I knocked on the office door and as it swung open, I saw my mother sitting down with *Little Nipper* in her hands. I immediately didn't feel well and couldn't move. I don't even think I took a breath.

Mrs. Hitchcock said, "Come in, Caroll."

I had to think who that was. I was null and void. I didn't know what to do.

My mother did though. She asked me if the flask was mine and I said, "Yes."

Then she said, "You didn't get this by yourself. Who gave it to you?"

I replied, "It's my Christmas present from Ray;" and then I cried.

Mrs. Hitchcock said that she had a very important question to ask me.

I said, "What is it you'd like to know?"

She asked me if I wanted to graduate from The Orchard.

I stood there and thought, "They're going to kick me out—three and a half years and now the ball game is over."

I said, "Yes, more than anything." (Where else could I go or get into?)

Mrs. Hitchcock said that she had had a long talk with

my mother, who was now taking out her handkerchief, and that as long as no other rules of the student's handbook were broken and if I did well on my finals, I could graduate from The Orchard.

It was heavy medicine but I felt like kneeling down and kissing the hem of her dress and then backing out of the office on my hands and knees.

Mother drove me home and I couldn't talk to her. She did all the talking anyway, enough for a whole radio show...all about the evils of liquor and how easy it is to become an alcoholic.

I asked her if I could have *Little Nipper* back. She didn't answer.

Willows Keep Bending

As the leaves fall, so the willow tree keeps bending its branches not to resist the breeze and so would Mrs. Lois Taylor. She could diminish a hurricane by acknowledging it, reacting to it in a diminutive way and yet keep flexible her own position while the only action she may have made was to slightly tap her pencil on a desk or table top. She was never uprooted.

Lois Taylor came to The Orchard my junior year and was our class English teacher as well as our homeroom teacher. She was neat, soft spoken, teaching almost as if she had been doing it for a hundred years and never without an appropriate response to any question. Her other specifics were that she lived on the Stanford campus and was married to an Associate Professor of English. He was thought to be cute by those who had seen him picking her up at school once or twice before she got her blue Volkswagon bug, sans radio. I guess Mrs. Taylor must have been about thirty years old.

Mrs. Taylor really put the junior class through its paces that year. We studied Shakespeare, the realm of Romantic English poets and Thomas Hardy. I was impressed with the course but never the first one in with my home-work assignments...in fact, often late.

Lois Taylor didn't admonish me in my fault of being late with papers. She, I think, sensed that I was just different and appreciated the fact that I listened and that I tried. I even think she knew me better than I knew myself because I would rather self destruct than fail or something like that and obviously needed extra help. I got extra coaching time... usually going over punctuation and simplifying sentences on papers that I had written for class. I never got any pre-preparation for examinations. The term exams were all left up to me and the clock.

It wasn't until I returned for my senior year, after Eu-rope, that I really felt Mrs. Taylor was interested in our class as individuals. She would be our homeroom and English teacher again, guiding us through Greek tragedies and college applications.

I guess it was about twice a month on Senior Day, when we could drive our cars, that members of the class got invited to drop by at Mrs. Taylor's. However, as I lived near-by the Stanford campus and really hadn't improved in turn-ing my papers in on time, she allowed me to drop them off at her house after school on the date due so I got to drive over by myself as well as with classmates.

Her house was charming...a small California Spanish style cottage with a tile roof and a little lawn out front. Her living room was comfortably cluttered with couches, canvas back chairs, tables with lots of periodicals on them and brass-based lamps with dark shades. There was one whole wall of bookshelves filled with an unlimited variety of books.

When I dropped off my paper on the character of Jocasta from *Oedipus Rex,* I remember asking her if she had ever been to Greece. She summoned me into the hallway and on into the kitchen and I watched her put flour on the pieces of liver that she was fixing for dinner. I wondered where the bacon was. I guess she could read my mind because she said, "Onions go so well with liver, don't you think?"

Well, no. I didn't think so because I could never digest onions...and I never found out if she had been to Greece or not.

The class had a seminar at Mrs. Taylor's towards the end of the year. It was quite an experience. We had our choice of coffee or tea and as many chocolate brownies as we could eat. This was the first time we had munchies offered to us.

I remember not having much to say as the topics were what our class gift to the school would be and what did we feel was the most rewarding subject covered in her class. I remember raising my hand for a *yes* vote on a wrought iron sign that said "The Orchard School" to be placed on a pillar of the porte-cochere but where it is today, I don't know. I do know that the class agreed that the most poignant subject discovered and explored in English 12 was that of the protagonists' characters.

All I could think of was how neat this was, being home entertained and I kept taking my spoon and filling it up with coffee grounds from the percolator on the end table near my seat and eating them. I really had a lot of *savoir-faire*.

Shortly afterwards, when we had to turn in our term thesis, I was late again and Mrs. Taylor said, when I popped mine by her door, "Oh, good, you got it in on time."

I really didn't want to come in but she seemed to suggest that it was all right. She let me sit in my favorite canvas back chair and this time it had a cushion on it, making it a softer seat. Gee, it was comfortable!

Mrs. Taylor started the conversation by telling me that she thought I had made great progress during the year and that she wanted me to know that she had enjoyed having me in her class.

Well, jeez, did I think I was something! But of course, I didn't believe it and let off my steam by saying, "Well, you see, we try harder."

She said, "Who's we?"

I remember saying, "Me, myself and I" and laughing. Yep, that was about it! I did try to believe but couldn't understand why anyone would pay me compliments. I always thought they were put-ons.

On that day we also talked about art. Lois Taylor said she "painted in oils" and I thought that was funny. Anyone else would have said that she did oil painting. About that time her husband came home from a lecture and Lois said, "Did you have a good class?"

He said, "Yes," and that he had stopped by the Tresidder Ticket Office and had gotten symphony tickets.

Gee, Lois looked happy. She excused herself, told me she would be right back and asked if I wanted coffee or tea.

I opted for the tea. She returned with an old-fashioned Bavarian china plate with little slices of brown bread with raisins and cream cheese spread on them. The tea was smooth and made the B & M New England Brown Bread go down easy.

Mrs. Taylor was something all right; you never knew just what she had up her sleeve and it was no wonder she was a favorite with all of her students.

I guess that's why, when I graduated, I never bothered to thank her. She must have known how we all felt, going on to places of higher education, new plateaus, that we had out-grown high school. But I saw a lot of tears at our graduation and still see them.

Me, I was just looking forward to going to the Fairmont Hotel for dinner and dancing with my date, Ray Douglas, and seeing Shelley Berman perform. Also, I knew that going with Ray would make it a special evening. After the dinner show, we trotted to every room in the hotel that featured drinks and cozy tables and talked about New York. I remember his telling me that there were people in New York who were probably out celebrating and talking about nothing except San Francisco.

I never said, "Good-bye" to The Orchard. I just dismissed it as my home town and thought someday I'd be back ...and, of course, all the faculty members would be there.

Four years later I graduated from a small, northern California college. I got a telephone call from a girlfriend who had transferred into The Orchard her senior year, Joanne Evert. She told me that Lois Taylor had passed away of cancer. She added that there was going to be a memorial service at the Stanford Chapel and that she wanted me to know because they were trying to get as many members of the class to be there as possible.

"Well, so be it," I told her. "I'm sorry to hear the news but I'm leaving for Yugoslavia and Greece tomorrow on a student tour...a graduation gift from my family. I'm sorry but I can't be there."

I hung up the phone and experienced anger first; it didn't seem fair. I repeated the question *Why?* I had no conclusion.

At least that got me to packing my suitcases. Afterwards I thought, "What can I do? Cancel my European trip? Of course not!" Then I started to cry, a whole flood of tears. Noah's ark could have floated on it.

I wanted to see Greece. Greece—I hadn't even given

that country a thought until we did those classics in English 12. That started off another chain reaction back to the total loss I had just heard about. My Grecian classic literature knowledge would have been zero if it hadn't been for Mrs. Taylor. Anyone else would have had us reading an American classic like *The Scarlet Letter,* not Mrs. Taylor. She had a world wide perspective.

There were tears pouring from my eyes and then just quiet. Well, at least that explained why she didn't teach last year and why it was passed off as doing research for her husband's publish or perish book.

I did feel an abiding friendship with Mrs. Taylor but I think a lot of her students felt the same. I think that was what was so special about her; she made *you* feel special. I wouldn't say she was introverted but her calm exterior, as if she knew what the world was all about and it couldn't dent her, sure gave a certain amount of serenity to the time spent with her. And yet, I did see moments of glee so I know she had a goodly amount of humor somewhere but it wasn't always apparent.

When I left on my European trip, a cruise down the Adriatic, and stopped at ports like Dubrovnik, all I could see was poverty and take pictures of it. I didn't want carved wood chess sets out of the store windows. I found myself amongst the city's fortifications and looking down narrow alleys and into windows and seeing everyone as Vincent Van Gogh's *Potato Eaters* sitting around a naked light bulb and eating or just sitting. I had a hole in my stomach with my gut down to my toes from loss. I took some super pictures of what seemed like super sorrow.

By the time the ship cruised down to the isles of Greece and made port at Piraeus for our three days in Athens, I was feeling better. I was experiencing the blaze of sun that belongs to Greece alone as far as I am concerned. Athens awakened me, walking and climbing the ruins, the Acropolis, and viewing the Parthenon were momentous aesthetic aphrodisiacs which turned my head from sorrow and towards the conviction that nothing is lost as long as there is memory.

However, if Athens turned me on, Delphi spawned me with horizons reaching beyond those of Athens and our tour had an excellent guide who talked under the stars about the very early Olympic Games. In the high altitude of Delphi, I truly felt its antiquity and knew the meaning of Apollo.

When I returned to the San Francisco Bay area in late August, I was getting ready for my first job after graduating from college, one I got through knowing the involved people. I went to work for the St. Mary's Cathedral Building Fund of San Francisco.

The job was good for a trainee who had never had an eight hour job before. It taught me how to count the checks that came in and to credit them to the correct accounts. After six months I was bored and knew it was time to pursue again the academic life. I sent for a Stanford University catalog and figured I would strive for a Bachelor of Science since I already had a Bachelor of Arts. The easiest trail was to go for a nursing career at Stanford which granted the Bachelor of Science degree and turned out administrative nurses. This sounded right up my line so I began taking entry requirements at San Mateo Junior College and the University of California at Berkeley.

My acceptance to Stanford brought back that chain of memories and I found time to visit the Park Florist, the best florist in Menlo Park. There I requested a fifteen inch laurel leaf wreath to be ready on a Saturday am.

I picked up my laurel wreath and signed a Bank-America charge slip for twenty-five dollars. I put the wreath on the back seat of my car and drove towards the Chasoregon Cemetery, fourteen miles south from Menlo Park.

I slowed down at the entrance and then parked my car in front of the administrative building. I walked in and over to the counter. There was a box of Kleenex lying on the desk. Well, this wasn't a crying time but I guess it would come in handy for others.

The attendant asked me if he could be of help.

I said, "Yes, I have this laurel wreath to deliver to a Mrs. B. Taylor's gravesite."

He asked, after looking up the reference in his card index, if her name was Lois Taylor.

I said, "Yes, that's the name."

He said that I could follow a driver to the plot site.

I thanked him and waited for the parade to begin. It was a sunny day but no activity around the cemetery, no funerals in process.

A rather chubby man got into a white car and drove slowly down a little avenue, made a right turn, then a left, stopped his car, got out and pointed across the way.

I waved at him, parked my car along the side of the curb and dragged out my fifteen inch laurel leaf wreath.

Before the guide left, he asked me what florist I was with. I told him I was delivering this for myself.

I found Lois Taylor's plot with no trouble. The stone said, *Beloved Wife of Bernard Taylor.* That was it and no doubt about it.

I stood there with my wreath resting against the headstone and had many thoughts. Well, so this is what it all boils down to.

Then I said out loud, "You deserve the best!"

I contemplated for a few minutes and then came up with some of the whimsical things that had crossed our lives.

I thought to myself, "Do you remember that letter that was addressed to Stanford and delivered to Hanford before it was sent back again to Stanford? It was the letter that I sent you from Albuquerque my sophomore year in college, explaining to you why I wanted to transfer to a small college. Don't you remember how we laughed at the address mix-up and how definite I was on getting back on the track of academics instead of staying at a 'drinking school'?

"I know you can't answer now, but I remember when I brought you the latest book I read and wanted to share with you and you said, 'It will be new to me but my husband has already read it' and that made me feel very unnecessary. I don't know if our shared experiences mean anything and I'll never know but sometime you'll know that what you shared with me will not go without some evidence."

I touched the laurel wreath that was now resting against the headstone and turned my back on the past but not without memory.

I was going to be the best nurse Stanford University had ever seen. The only problem was that I was geared for the aesthetic life with scientific principles but not scientific practices...I couldn't take patient's pulses!

After one summer's experience on the Stanford Hospital's payroll, I resigned and went to work for the University's Bowman Alumni House. I was back to opening envelopes and counting money and crediting accounts. Business always goes on.

The Geranium Buds

I think it was in the early 1970's that I received the last of the wedding announcements of friends (including Howard Hewitt's) whom I was sure that I was going to beat down the aisle. All of a sudden, ninety-eight percent of my friends were married. Of course, not that many had been around the world or had parents who paid for an American Express trip such as I had. The only thing it cost me was my job at Stanford. They granted two weeks vaction, not four, and it was no surprise that my receptionist job at the Faculty Club had gone to my substitute.

I lived with my parents because it was the most practical thing to do. They had a large house and though the rooms all had collectables in them, we never felt squeezed for space. Mother kept house like a Victorian with little or no planning as to special collections of art. If she had a piece of Steuben glassware on a table, next to it would be a ceramic of a crazy cat made in Japan and bought at Cost Plus. Whenever I asked her why she brought home such things, she had one standard reply: "I liked it and this is *my* home."

I certainly didn't feel the most comfortable not having a job and staying around her house all day but I couldn't see spending money to rent an apartment—just money going out...when maybe I could help Mother get organized.

So each day started off with breakfast and as there wasn't much to do without any of Mother's instructions, I stayed at the breakfast table until it was time for lunch. Out of boredom, I ate breakfast cereal by the box, thinking that with my stomach full, I could work better. But there was nothing Mother wanted worked on. She watched me eat the cereals, brought more from the store to fill the empty cupboard and when they were gone, bought more. I finally tipped the scale twenty pounds heavier than I had been and that was it.

Obviously, Mother liked me in the breakfast room eating and being home. I didn't and told her that I'd had it, that she never was going to go through her collections and that she wouldn't live long enough to see her clothes and shoes come back into style! All she said was, "Do you want some apricot nectar?"

I began to be a patio poolside lounger. I looked at job advertisements in the newspaper. That was about all I did: look, get disgusted, do forty laps in the pool and lounge again in the sun.

One afternoon Mother came out to the poolside and said that if I thought *I* was in bad shape, she knew a boy who had gone blind from diabetes just when he had announced his engagement. The families had called off the ceremony and I should realize how lucky I was that I wasn't blind.

"Yes," I thought. I was lucky and agreed with her. Mother was really good at heart breaking stories. She had written a whole book of heart breaking poems so I knew what she was going to suggest next.

"Why don't you call Tim and introduce yourself? I'm sure he would like to hear a sweet voice and besides, you don't know what it's like to be dying."

"Who's Tim?" I said.

"He's Bee's son," she said.

"Bee who?" I said.

"Bee Towner, a friend of Ellen's. Tim is Bee's younger son. I saw him the other day. He is a beautiful boy and so clean in mind and spirit. They're Mormons and have great faith. Bee told me that Tim is in and out of the hospital so very often now because of his advanced diabetes. He has had it since he was eight years old," Mother said, really touched.

"How old is he now?" I asked.

"He's twenty-six," she replied.

"Are you sure he's dying?" I asked with caution.

"Well, none of us is sure of anything but Bee told me that they were resigned to the bare facts of the disease," Mother declared.

"Well, I'm not doing anymore Florence Nightingale work. I did my time," I declared.

"When?" Mother asked.

I just looked away and let my eyes fall downwards and thought that that was the biggest hang-up with my folks: they could never see the good things I'd done, only the absurdities.

"I didn't say you were to do anything except be your sweet self and maybe offer a little company to this beautiful boy. I don't suppose you would know anything about how it feels to have to face such a disease and its consequences," she said firmly.

I replied that maybe I did but I didn't want to be around anyone who was depressed.

Mother said that she didn't notice any depression as

he had great faith and was making a lot of adjustments and had been to school for the blind.

I remember telling Mother that I knew a lot about adjustments and that the next time she and Dad took me to the World's Exposition in Japan and let me see how a million people adjusted to 103° of temperature that I'd talk to her about adjustments.

"What are you talking about? You had a lovely trip," she counterpointed.

"It cost me my job," I said.

"You don't have to work, you know," she probed.

I looked at her and remembered when she said, "You don't have to go to college if you don't want to" and my father had a Phi Beta Kappa key.

"Well, if I don't go to work, what do you think I should do?" I said.

"You could give a little of yourself to someone who is less fortunate than yourself," she concluded.

The next day I decided to give Tim Towner a telephone call; maybe we could discuss music. I dialed his home number, introduced myself to Bee Towner and asked to speak to Tim. Bee seemed happy that I had called and after a couple of minutes, Tim came to the phone.

"Hello, I'm Caroll, one of your friendly neighbors," I said.

Tim's voice was low and precise and he asked me where I went to school. Had I gone to Menlo High School?

"No," I said. "I went to one of those private girls' schools where you wear uniforms and can't wait until the weekends when you go out on a date."

This seemed to tickle Tim's sense of humor. He told me that he was a Mormon and that after he had done his missionary work, he had gotten a job at the Stanford Computation Center as a messenger boy."

I said that I had also worked at Stanford. I could tell that there was an intellectual gap between us and I did not tell him that I had gone to the University for post graduate work.

Tim was very game on the phone and we arranged a meeting between the two of us. He suggested that I come over on Saturday afternoon as he had no doctors' appointments and was free.

I asked him if he liked music and he said that he did but not acid rock or the heavy classics.

I thought, "Good. We are even on that score." Then he said that he had just gotten an album that he liked very much and wondered if I had heard it. It was called *Paint Your Wagon*.

I went over on Saturday to introduce myself and visit with Tim. There wasn't a lot to say. He was a diabetic and had to take some nourishment on a special schedule. He was blond, rosy cheeked, a beautiful young man just as Mother had said. He told me that he didn't want a guide dog to help him get around and that he could do better with a cane and a person to watch over him.

I remember staying close to the subject of music and asked him to play *Paint Your Wagon*. It was from the movie's soundtrack, its theme, early pioneering days. Tim obliged me; put the record on the stereo and then settled back in a living room chair to enjoy the music. I guess in the six weeks that I knew Tim we listened to that album twelve times. It would have done me little or no good to suggest *South Pacific* since Tim knew what he liked and what he didn't like. I think, also, that he knew his time was running out.

There were afternoons when I would go over to Tim's house and visit, have a cracker and cheese and read to him from *The Book of the American West.* He really enjoyed the whole early American scene. Me, I would have been asking for Hemingway. However, we read chapters on *Transportation to the West* and *Indians and Soldiers of the American West.* One time he commented that he wished I could partake in the Mormon movement and that his friends and he would teach me about Mormonism.

I left his house very perturbed. When I got home, I told Mother what this whole friendship had gotten me into. I said, "Tim wants me to take classes in the evening with his Mormon friends so that I will know about the *Book of Mormon.*

Mother said, "Well, you don't have to if you don't want to but, remember, it's his way and if you could console him by participating in the seminar, it probably wouldn't hurt you."

"But, I'm not going to be a Mormon. Gads! It's all I can do to understand my own faith without changing my stripes completely," I said.

Then Mother informed me that she was going down to Orange County to take care of her younger brother who was alone and suffering from multiple sclerosis. She wanted to arrange decent household help and she didn't know how long she'd be gone. It would be up to me to look after my father.

Once again Mother started things but had no way of seeing my future except for what was immediately necessary.

I thought about Tim's suggestion and agreed with Mother that a little exposure to different ways of doing things wouldn't hurt me. Also, it would be nice to meet some people my own age. And, I think, more than anything else, Tim's situation had touched me so that if he wanted me to read to him about Joseph Smith, I would have responded truly.

He had Mormon missionaries come over to his house twice a week and so it was there that I would be sitting next to Tim, pleasant, and with questions about the fundamentals of their faith. Tim really enjoyed these times. He was being involved with final blooms of life's meaning to him.

One evening after the missionaries left, Tim said that he wanted to take a day's round trip plane ride to somewhere and wanted to know if I would go with him.

I was surprised but not without a suggestion as to where we should go. I said that I had an aunt in Long Beach. It might be fun to fly down in the morning, have lunch with her and then fly back to San Francisco. Tim liked the idea and told his mother. Bee told me that it would certainly be an outing that Tim would enjoy and that she hoped it would work out.

I left Tim's house and when I got home, I found my father reading the newspaper in his favorite chair in the den. I told him of Tim's wish and he said, "Fine. Call your Aunt Marjorie and find out what would be a good day. Just be sure to be home by dinner time."

I had been cooking dinner for Dad and myself and being calorie conscious, he got the *Blue Plate Special* and I got the salad. It was fun making dinner for someone else and we'd watch the evening news while we ate. It was almost like being at the Douglas's. I really missed them since they moved away but this was every bit as good.

The day came when Tim with his white cane and I walked through the San Francisco Airport, checked in and got on the Western Airlines flight to Long Beach. He didn't wear dark glasses and his sunny face shown with happiness. The flight attendants were happy to help us find our seats. It was a short flight, just a little over an hour. As it was an early morning flight, Tim didn't need any of his special diet foods.

They had coffee and other beverages available on the plane but we didn't indulge. We would be having an early lunch with my aunt who was going to meet us at the airport. The flight was a smooth one.

Aunt Marjorie was there. After introductions, we got into her Volkswagon station wagon and departed from the airport. I had already talked to her about Tim's blindness and diabetic condition. She drove us right out to Seaport Village where Tim could feel the sea air and that strange combination of fog and sultriness which belongs to Long Beach. We all decided on *The Jolly Roger* restaurant as a good choice because there were a variety of items on the menu as opposed to going to *Jose Pete's* which served Mexican food only.

We had a delightful lunch. I only had to tell Tim what was on his plate as if it were the face of a clock and he managed to find everything he wanted. Aunt Marjorie and I had our usual running conversation about her pets. She is a cat fancier and has about six or seven permanent residents along with two or three who freeload from the alley.

After Tim paid the check for our lunches, we walked through the little shopping plaza and did some browsing at a card shop. I read him some of the contemporary cards. Aunt Marjorie wanted to look for some special culinary tool at a boutique for kitchen items...and so our time went.

Tim and I were chauffeured to Long Beach Airport by Aunt Marjorie. We both thanked her and headed towards gate three and Western Airlines for the return flight to San Francisco just as if we were old hands at this jet set way of life.

That was Tim's last plane ride. I guess it was about a week later that I had a strange feeling about the way the leaves were falling and the acorns dropping on our driveway in Atherton. I decided to call an alumna friend from The

Orchard, Joanne Evert, and ask her what she was up to.

Joanne was happy to hear from me and glad to fill me in on the news that she was going for her Masters in Geography. I piped up that I was being a "housekeeper" and thinking about a job after my mother got back from southern California.

I hung up and stared at the phone. Joanne was happy and going to school. I was not happy and staying at home with my parents. I had a worthless feeling.

Later that day Bee called me and told me that Tim was in the Stanford Hospital. She said that the doctors were concerned about his metabolism and his blood pressure and that if I wanted to visit him it probably should be soon.

I said that I understood and that evening, before Father was expected home, I went over to the hospital and saw Tim for the last time. Bee was there and Tim's older brother and his father. I went to Tim's bedside and touched his hand and told him that he was loved and kissed him on the forehead. He didn't talk but I think he knew it was me.

Bee thanked me for coming. I said that I wanted to and meant it. Tim was a very beautiful young man and the purity of his beliefs rested on love and not pride.

When Dad got home, I told him all about my day. I fixed dinner and asked him if he thought I should go back to school and maybe take accounting. He said that was about the only thing I hadn't taken up and wondered what I would do with it afterwards. I said, "I'd get a job."

He replied with a grin, "Well, maybe I could fit you in at my company."

"What would I do?" I said.

"Oh, we'll think of something for you to do," he said confidently.

"Like what?" I persisted.

"Sara left and we have no one to be the receptionist or operate the switchboard; the girls are taking turns."

"I guess I could do that all right. How much does it pay?"

The Rabbit's Foot Fern

I drove my Capri into the drive around Oak Woods where my condominium is and stopped. I got out and opened the garage door, leaving my extra parking space for Michael's red Porsche. I unlatched the black, wrought iron gate that told me I was entering another world...a beautifully land-scaped area with an oval swimming pool, umbrellas and chairs and patches of lawn overseen by a gigantic oak tree, some pines and redwoods.

I felt that this was my Shangri La all except for the nagging neighbor living below me who didn't like disco music and would thump the chair every time the noise level reached her. She would also put on her raincoat, stand on her small, fenced off patio and shout up to me while I was watering my potted plants that the water was just streaming down on her from my deck to her patio and that she was trying to dry things out. I would look down and never see any damage except trickles of water on her patio cement. Her name was Helen. It really was and she was the major distraction in my solitary Shangri-La.

Oh well, Michael would be here in a half hour, just time to open the freezer and select something from an assort ment of Stouffer's finely prepared frozen dinner delights. I put my key in the dead lock, then the doorknob and was home. I knew Michael would bring some wine so I'd wait for him before having a drink. I decided to change clothes. No use wearing a dress since I'd be cooking dinner home. I put on my red slacks, blue turtleneck and white over-blouse. I was comfortable with Maine loafers instead of high heels. It was time to kick-back and relax.

I walked through my living room, checked for sur-faces that needed dusting, rearranged my coffee table, placed a paperback book, Aldous Huxley's *Chrome Yellow* on top of a University of New Mexico Alumnus Report and whisked away a corporation's report to shareholders which had been updated by a new quarterly report. I was momentarily unde-cided as to what to do with the needlepoint design with its strands of yarn separated into various colors but decided to leave it in motion.

Michael liked the shimmer of intellectual things. He enjoyed games, as I do, but rarely beat me at Backgammon. We learned together, introducing each other to the favorites in our own worlds. I discovered how many people are really into science fiction and know the cult's realm of authors. I learned that bicycle riding has become a very classy sport with special wheels and pedals. Last, but not least, we both shared an ear for country music. We enjoyed each other's company with no strings.

Tonight, I decided to select my Crystal Gale albums for cocktails and dinner music background for the evening. The phone rang. It was Michael. He told me how sorry he was but he had to work at the store that night and he wouldn't be coming down to the peninsula.

I asked him why he had to work when he had been there all day.

He said, "The Chinaman couldn't come in to work because of a fever."

I asked him how he could be there eight hours during the day and be expected to fill in for someone until nine pm.

Michael just said, "Some days you're lucky and some-- times you get the rug pulled out from under your feet."

I asked him when we could get together since tonight was out and he lived two hours away.

He just hemmed and said that he'd call me and that he was sorry about tonight.

Darn it! So was I. Fooling around with an unpredictable Sears insurance man wasn't my idea of a big plus. I liked independent men, men who didn't have to run to answer a bell. But I did understand.

I started to think about putting one of the Stouffer's dinners back into the freezer before it thawed out and also that it was time to water my house plants. The weather had been in the middle 70's so it was probably time to give all thirteen household plants a little thirst quencher.

I was watering my Rabbit's Foot fern when the phone rang again. I let it ring three times before I had my hands free to reach it. When I answered, a far away voice said, "Caroll?"

I said, "Yes."

"This is Lance Conrad" came over the wires.

"Lance," I said, breathless. "Where are you?"

"I'm at the Hilton Inn at the San Francisco Airport."

"What are you doing in California? I thought that after you moved to Aspen, you would never come back."

"You know, I am still separated from my wife."

I said I was sorry to hear that and asked him how his store was doing.

" 'Skiers and Hikers' is doing so well that I may sell it."

I wished him all the success in the world.

He asked me if I had been to any Stanford soccer games lately.

I reflected on all the soccer games we had gone to when he was assisting the soccer coach at Stanford.

I said, "No, but I like football."

He said, "What kind of a team have you got for this season?"

I said, "Well, the coach is new; the quarterback is new; the running backs are untried. Sort of seems like it's going to be a dark horse."

Lance laughed and then he asked what I was doing this evening.

I replied that I was having ten people in for dinner with strip poker to follow.

Lance laughed again and then told me that he had rented a car and would like to take me out to the *49er's Club* for drinks and dinner.

I agreed and said that I would like very much to see him.

He had been one of the most fascinating men I had known. He had graduated from Harvard and when I was going with him had had a silver Mercedes with a telephone in it.

Lance was always telling me that I should be making use of my history and art history field instead of working at Dwyer Grader Blades, my father's plant. He always used to ask me what they were for—tractors? I'd reply that we preferred the term motor graders and sold a lot to California and Nevada. Then he'd tell me again that I should be doing something besides office work with my talents. I would then feel self-conscious and explain to him that I had never gone after a teaching credential and had worked up to a nice position. It paid well and included a new car with paid insurance. Lance then would cap off the topic by asking me when I was going to take over my father's business. I'd answer him by being straight forward and telling him I liked working in the business world and that at the plant I could be useful to my family after all they had done for me. It's not like working for something that isn't partly yours I'd say.

So, I had a date with Lance Conrad tonight. I chucked the remaining Stouffer's dinner back into the freezer and went into my bedroom to change clothes. I looked through my closet and decided on a white skirt and a red scoop neck jersey top.

I caught sight of my face in the mirror and stared at it. How long had it been since I'd gone out with Lance? Two years, I reflected. The biggest change was having to look at one of my anterior teeth that had turned brown. I was definitely going to have it pulled or capped.

On the far wall was a picture of a younger, smiling me and my fiance. We had parted soon thereafter; I had wanted children and he had not. It would be three years next week since the engagement had been broken off.

I looked into the mirror again and said to myself, "You know, Caroll, it's not going to be too much longer and you're going to be a member of the 39er's Club."

I froze and then thought that would probably not be so bad and that I was silly to think negatively. I'd had my chance at the bridal bouquet and had made my choice.

Gathering Garlands
Light the Laurels